In the pantheon of artists, a few individuals possess transcendent ability and vision. With hands, mind, and spirit, these larger-than-life artists create work of universal significance. As artists they inspire imitators. As visionaries, they capture the public's imagination. As leaders, they generate the symbols of their times.

Mastery & Meaning offers an intimate look at the extraordinary paintings created by Nelson Shanks, who orchestrates color, draftsmanship and insight with consummate flair. He has dedicated his life not only to creating art with the sure touch of a master, but to collecting it with the astute eye of a connoisseur, and to nurturing countless students with generosity and open-hearted instruction.

The Abraham Lincoln Foundation of the Union League is proud to present *Mastery & Meaning*, the first significant public display of art at the esteemed League House in more than a century. This exhibition is the first to focus on the works of a single artist. The Union League of Philadelphia has served as a center for culture since its inception in 1862. This exhibition is funded in part by the Commonwealth of Pennsylvania, Department of Community and Economic Development.

Mastery & Meaning

The Paintings of
Nelson Shanks

THE UNION LEAGUE OF PHILADELPHIA

Published on the occasion of the exhibition *Mastery & Meaning*,
sponsored by The Abraham Lincoln Foundation of The Union League of Philadelphia.

Exhibition dates
October 7, 2006 to December 17, 2006

This project was financed in part by a grant from the
Commonwealth of Pennsylvania, Department of Community and Economic Development.

Anne Emerson Hall, catalog editor.

Cover

"PIGTAILS"

2004; oil on canvas; 20 x 28 inches

James A. Michener Art Museum

Museum purchase with funds provided by the Janus Society

Frontispiece

"PERSONA"

2005; oil on canvas; 24 x 18 inches

Larry and Anne Hall Collection

Persona presents many faces of the painter Nelson Shanks. "The figureheads and objets d'art *represent moods and attitudes associated with myself. The model may be responding to those ideas but she hides her face, so we can't be sure."*

ISBN-13: 978-1-933086-01-9

ISBN-10: 1-933086-01-7

CONTENTS

The Commonwealth of Pennsylvania has been the birthplace of a remarkable array of gifts to the world during our 300-year history. These gifts range from some of the most important political moments in world history, to epic battles that created and saved our nation, to cultural and artistic gifts that enrich the lives of the commonwealth and the nation. As governor, I am pleased to introduce a gift from our commonwealth that is sure to inspire and captivate all who view it: *Mastery & Meaning*. This wonderful exhibit brings together one of the most important artists of our time, Nelson Shanks, with The Union League of Philadelphia, one of the most important private institutions in our Commonwealth's history.

In June of this year it was my privilege to honor Nelson Shanks with the Distinguished Arts Award, recognizing his significant contribution through his art and teaching. Working from his Bucks County home and studio during the last three decades, Nelson has created a vast body of work whose artistic value and renown enriches both Pennsylvania and the Nation. His lifelong commitment to teaching inspired him to make another invaluable contribution to the strength and vitality of our time with the founding of Studio Incamminati in Center City Philadelphia.

Nelson has proclaimed, "If our culture is what we leave for posterity, then together we can touch immortality by creating that which makes us proud." It is his purpose that Studio Incamminati foster a movement to create richly meaningful art for the benefit of civilization. Given the remarkable examples presented in his body of work, I have full confidence that he and his students will fulfill this claim.

I hope you will share my pride and pleasure in looking at the paintings created by Nelson Shanks. It is my further hope that you will join in the spirit of creativity and purpose that this exhibition represents for the future of us all, including the Union League, the City of Philadelphia, the Commonwealth of Pennsylvania, and our descendants.

COMMONWEALTH OF PENNSYLVANIA
THE GOVERNOR

EDWARD G. RENDELL
Governor

Mastery & Meaning Steering Committee

Dianne Semingson, Co-chair
Diane Dalto Woosnam, Co-chair
Howard Aaronson
Shirley Bonnem
David Cassedy
Patricia Connolly
Dorothy Giordano Housel
Leslie Swinney Kase
Linda R. Knox
John J. Meko, Jr.
Patricia D. Tobin

Abraham Lincoln Foundation Staff

John J. Meko, Jr.,
Executive Director

David Cassedy,
Curator of Art

Leslie Swinney-Kase,
Director of Institutional Advancement

James Mundy,
Director of Library & Historical Collections

The Union League of Philadelphia was founded in 1862, first and foremost, to help insure the preservation of the Union and support the Lincoln administration and its actions during the Civil War. Still, arts and culture were never far from the minds of its members, for they constituted the leadership for most of the major cultural organizations of the time. As individuals they were also the cornerstone of financial support for those organizations. Today, the membership of the Union League includes over 3,100 members. As they did in 1862, today's members represent the Philadelphia region's leaders in business, education, religion, the arts and culture.

Given the extent of the members' cultural interest, it is not surprising that the League House itself became a primary venue for public art exhibitions. The first exhibit was presented in 1870, and over the next thirty years, numerous exhibitions were held; sometimes several in a single year. These exhibitions were some of the most important and critically acclaimed artistic events in the country during the later half of the 19th century and including works by the great living American masters such as Thomas Sully, Thomas Moran, Rembrandt Peale, Xanthus Smith and Henry Naegle. European masters included Tissot, Millet, Monet and Pissaro. The largest, which was held in 1893, included over 300 paintings loaned from private collections of League's members. The last public art exhibition was held at the League more than 100 years ago.

Mastery & Meaning reestablishes this important League tradition, and adds a new chapter in this history as the first exhibition featuring a single artist, Nelson Shanks. Through *Mastery & Meaning*, The Abraham Lincoln Foundation invites the public into the League House to view the masterworks of Nelson Shanks and to experience the fine arts collection and architecture of the Union League. It is our hope that guests will be inspired by the beauty and significance of the art, as well as the ideals and spirit of the League as epitomized by our motto, "Love of Country Leads." This motto commits the League and its members to being active and visible business, educational, cultural, and civic leaders. The Foundation and the League believe that this exhibit of Nelson Shanks' artwork will inspire, and create opportunities for meaningful interaction between the League and the greater Philadelphia community.

On behalf of the Union League of Philadelphia and the Abraham Lincoln Foundation, I welcome you to the League House, and to *Mastery & Meaning*.

James B Straw

JAMES B. STRAW
Chairman of the Board of Trustees

SELF-PORTRAIT

1987, oil on canvas; 22 x 30 inches

Collection of the artist

Mastery & Meaning

Nelson Shanks and Humanist Realism

Nelson Shanks is the preeminent realist painter of our time, a true master of his craft and a penetrating interpreter of the human condition. His technical skill and exceptional command of color combine to produce canvases that mine the human condition and bring fresh, vibrant meanings to our world, all the while reminding us that there remains in our world things beautiful. As the works in this catalogue attest, Shanks' realism is profoundly humanistic. The many portraits in this catalogue are best understood as explorations of the human soul that reveal profound and moving things about who we are and what we hope to be. Art, it has been said, is a lie that speaks to a great truth. Such is the case with Nelson Shanks.

Among Shanks' teachers were Henry Hensche, John Koch, Robert Brackman, Ivan Olinsky and Edwin Dickinson. To them he owes a great debt. He honors their legacy by continuing to teach aspiring artists to become artists in their own right. But in many ways Shanks was self-taught. By the time his interest in art blossomed, realist painting of any stripe had fallen in disfavor. Devotees of modernism, broadly understood, had rebelled against the very technical skill Shanks yearned to develop, presuming craftsmanship a fetter on creativity. Cultural sophisticates were likewise drawn to modernism in all its avant garde manifestations, insisting in the process that art had no boundaries, that historical standards of artistic excellence were artificial, and that virtually anything could be considered "art." Shanks thought otherwise. Just as one could not presume to write creatively without first mastering language, Shanks understood that mastery of the craft of painting was prerequisite for artistic expression, and that technique, rather than restrict the artist, liberated him or her. But there were very few people to whom he could turn for instruction. What Shanks did to hone his skills was initiate a dynamic dialogue with the Old Masters and selected impressionists. He spent countless hours in museums and churches sketching masterpieces of the past in hopes of generating a realism relevant to the present and future. His success in using the past to add fresh meaning to the present has been remarkable.

Shanks' dialogue with the past and his steadfast commitment to technique are basic to his artistic creativity, which is not to be confused with artistic innovation. Much of modernism was – and is – driven by the cult of novelty, often imbued with transgressive political content intended to shock rather than educate in language lacking nuance, sophistication and subtlety. But endlessly innovative art – the reigning orthodoxy throughout Shanks' career – is self-immolating, and the compulsion to shock has worn thin on a public now accustomed to the outrageous. And now that we know the outrageous sells well, the political intent of so much modernist work has become a parody of itself: the avant garde has out-commodified the hated bourgeoisie.

The heterodox Shanks, in contrast, wants to extend the past, not escape from it, and he aspires to create an enduring art that reveals and affirms something about the human condition qua human condition. Shanks does not so much record life; he penetrates its complexities. His realism is not a reproduction but an unpacking of life. Shanks' work shows us that there is something about the human being that is greater than the sum of its parts. He shows us facets of the human experience that are essential, not existential. That Shanks paints primarily by the north light speaks to this very point. (He also deploys artificial light as examples in this catalogue attest.) The north light, in contrast to the southern, offers consistent illumination of the object of study. With northern light the artist can identify intently with the object of study, which is presumed to have a reality as such. Southern light is too variable, altering the object of study as the painting day unfolds. It does not allow for the intense communion of the artist with the object of study, a communion necessary for the mining of something essential.

Southern light was favored by those who ushered in the artistic revolution that was modernism. It resonated with their relativistic assumptions about reality and existential nature of human selves. According to this view, nothing about our cultural reality, including works of art, transcends time and place, and there exists nothing essential about man to capture on canvas. Art is simply culture-bound, a manifestation of particular localities which cannot speak to universal themes of human experience because no such themes exist. In turn, human beings are infinitely malleable, forever changing with the roles they assume in everyday life, roles apart from which selves have no basis. The long-held conviction that basic to our humanity was a transcendent nature accessible to human reason and the human eye was rejected out of hand.

Shanks insisted this view was misguided. His own studies of art history suggested as much. After all, who today, regardless of religious identity, can study the great Bruges Masters of the 14th and 15th centuries and not be moved by the human emotion they convey? Who can study the great Bolognese artists of the 16th and 17th centuries and not be touched by their power and beauty? How was it that in preparation for a recent show of Raphael's work, curators wept as they hung the work of the great master? These are not cultural artifacts but monuments to the human experience that speak to us with great force, at least those of us who remain open to the possibility that man is not simply the summation of the roles he assumes in everyday life. They continue to direct us towards a more complete understanding – and appreciation – of the human experience. They continue to inspire.

Reproduced in this catalogue are examples of Shanks' work spanning some three decades. Many of these works are included in the exhibition hosted by the Abraham Lincoln Foundation at the Union League of Philadelphia. They include still life, landscape, allegories, and portraits. Together they convey the complexity of the human experience with great force. The portrait of the late John Paul II is a case in point. Here Shanks has captured the transcendent spirituality of his subject. The canvas is not simply a recording of the great Pontiff but a penetrating look into the complex spiritual yearning of a man whose presence so captivated millions, Catholic and non-Catholic alike. We actually feel the power of his presence as he stands in the Basilica, his right hand raised in blessing. And, let us not forget, it is Shanks' superb draftsmanship and extraordinary command of color that drive the power of this image. Technique mines the soul.

Mr. Fitting, the earliest example in this exhibition, shows Shanks at his best in probing the psychology of the human subject. Intensely introspective, *Mr. Fitting* invites us to explore with him the complexities of the human condition through the life course. Equally moving are Shanks' treatment of *J. Carter Brown*, the late director of the National Gallery in Washington, and his sketch of the tenor *Luciano Pavarotti*. In these examples Shanks captures a certain passion that arrests our attention and that invite us once again to share human emotion with the subjects themselves. We are compelled to feel the intensity evident in the portrayal of Brown and to touch the lyricism emanating from Pavarotti. And so it is with all of Shanks' studies of human character. *Anne Faulkner Schoemaker*, *William Jefferson Clinton*, *Michael*

Bloomberg, Mary McFadden, Diana, and the many other examples of portraiture reproduced here evoke in us commonly held emotions and experiences, no matter how illustrious, famous or powerful the subject is. These penetrating examinations of the human being restore the great tradition of portraiture to its rightful place among the fine arts.

Shanks' intimate articulations of the human psyche stand in contrast to the monumental allegory *Sophia, (An Anthology).* Sophia stands before us enigmatically; she is at once confident and vulnerable. Arranged around her are objects from everyday life, from the coffee can to the pumpkin mask, the interpretation of which Shanks has left to our own devices. We are invited to explore the image of a life, both comic and tragic, as all lives are.

The deployment of everyday objects is common in Shanks' work. *Fortune Teller,* for example, and *Pumpkin* are among studies where Shanks uses the common to construct a symbolic world we are then asked to interpret. The use of the everyday speaks to Shanks' humor. Works such as *Pumpkin* or *Pigtails* cannot help but elicit pleasure. But often Shanks juxtaposes commonplace elements to suggest something not at all routine, for instance, the strongly – and strangely – symbolic *Persona.*

Perhaps no canvas conveys as strongly Shanks' artistic commitments as the allegory of painting *"Incamminati", Personification of Painting.* This triumphant declaration of artistic integrity announces the founding of Studio Incamminati, an art school inspired by the Carracci academy of the same name, brought to fruition in Philadelphia by Shanks himself. The figure, boldly modeled, gazes at us with confidence, even defiance, as she strides forward, progressing, as it were, which is the literal meaning of "incamminati." She is the embodiment of art, properly understood, a constructive movement challenging the transgressive modernism that so defined the 20th century. Her energy is echoed by the restless noble steed positioned in the rear of the canvas. She heralds a brighter future where art illuminates and instructs rather than conceals and obfuscates. This is how Shanks understands his own genre of art.

Examples of Shanks' still life work includes the compelling *What Have We Done to Angels.* This is none too subtle commentary on the cultural impoverishment of our times. The exquisitely rendered angel hangs from a gallows, her head turned to the side, as if in shame, hiding from our gaze. Behind the angel floats a red ribbon, running horizontally on the canvas, a ribbon that conceals the head of a putto situated in the background. The easel evokes a sacrificial cross. The angel hangs not from rope but from a modern metal wire, and her garment is held together by a paper clip. The metal wire and paper clip are harsh images that stand in stark contrast to the angel and what the angel represents. Here Shanks brings into view the profanation of American life, the assault on things beautiful. This assault is multi-faceted, coming not only from certain quarters of modern art, examples of which a recent critic has aptly labeled "deathworks," but from our fixation on technology as well and our unwillingness to confront a world where the technical control of conditions serves no higher purpose save technical control. *What Have We Done to Angels* is Shanks' siren call.

Shanks thereby reminds us that the profanation of life is something to resist. And resist we should, as there remains in our world things that are truly beautiful, if one has the eye to see them and the courage to bring them forward. Thematically, what runs throughout the corpus of Shanks' work is the reminder that surrounding us are things that inspire. To wit: The exquisite still life *Danilova's Slipper* transforms a simple ballet slipper into an object of aesthetic delight. The series of studies entitled *Laura,* and works such as *Flora* and *Peacock,* driven as they are by remarkable command of color, move the soul. (How often do we stop and admire the color about us?) *Catalina Island* evokes a natural world that is dream-like. And Shanks' sensual rendering of fabric in any number of paintings manifests an astonishing gift in rendering beautiful what many of us regard as common place.

In the end Shanks' work is fruit for the mind and soul. He pushes the intellect as he delights our aesthetic sense. Just as he developed as an artist by immersing himself in the best thinking of past centuries, he now pushes thinking forward in our time by achieving more with eye and hand than ever thought possible. We are fortunate to have among us an artist who regards his craft constructively and whose sharing of his great gifts enriches our lives.

James R. Abbott, Ph.D.

Part I

Icons

Icons of our age are public figures, whose images pervade modern media and create a sense of familiarity with them. Yet we hope that there is, indeed, more there than meets the eye. When Nelson Shanks takes on the task to paint them, we can see what we have not seen before. We see why if not how the artist triumphs over the technician. He is able with open eye, heart and mind to see beneath the recognizable surface to greater truths and with consummate deftness to convey the experience of genuine contact with a living person.

His portrayals meet needs far deeper than the immediate thrill of journalistic voyeurism, because they help us to see more deeply, to sense what makes a person tick. Captured here are feelings of presence far more lasting than the moment a shutter clicks or the record button is pressed—the difference between the timeless and the momentary image and thought.

"Shanks' portrayal of Pope John Paul II is a work of great sympathy and insight and will be our most enduring painted image of one of the preeminent religious and historical figures of [the 20th] century."

D. Dodge Thompson
Director of Exhibitions
National Gallery, Washington, DC

Portrait of His Holiness, John Paul II

2002; oil on canvas; 54 x 50 inches

Art Heritage Holdings LLC

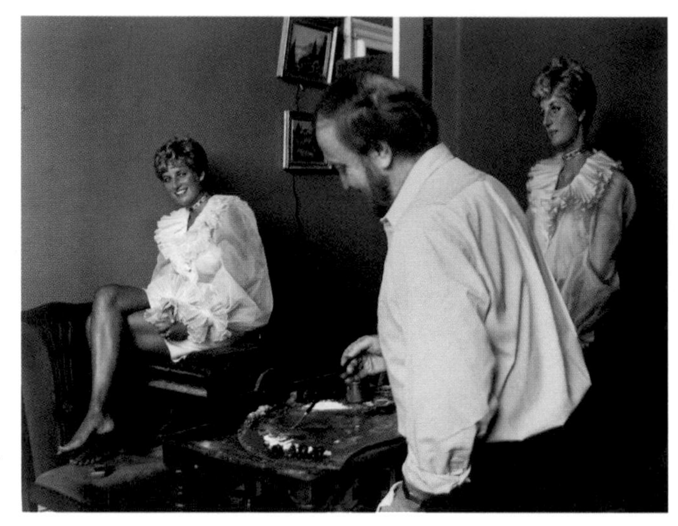

Photo by Leona Shanks

"If there is anything that is wonderful and warm and human and open that you could imagine about her, it is true. An absolutely spectacular person under great stress."

Nelson Shanks

Portrait of H.R.H., Diana, Princess of Wales

1994; oil on canvas; 64 x 40 inches

Collection of Charles, Ninth Earl Spencer
Althorp, Northamptonshire, England

"The greatest cellist and one of the greatest musicians of all times."

Jeremy Eichler, The New York Times

"Mstislav Rostropovich is the world ambassador of classical music — the last of that generation who can communicate music's wonder. He's like my grandfather. He's my hero. And I call him my angel, because he supports me as a mentor...Musically, Rostropovich is the link for younger generations to such geniuses as Sergei Profokiev and Dmitri Shostakovich...He really understands what music means.

"He has taught me not to force my personality into a work, but instead try to touch the spirit of the composer; then the audience can connect with the music's universal emotion...His work [vaccinating nearly 2 million children across Russia] symbolizes all that is great about the Russian soul...Generations have been touched by his miraculous spirit, and will continue to be touched long after he is gone."

Maxim Vengerov,
Star classical violinist and protégé of Rostropovich

Mstislav Rostropovich

2006; oil on canvas; 62 x 51 inches

Lent by Ian and Annette Cumming

"Denyce Graves is particularly well-known for her signature portrayals of the title roles in Carmen *and* Samson et Dalila, *both of which partnered her with the great Placido Domingo, among others."*

UCLA Today

Nelson Shanks painted the soprano Denyce Graves in the dramatic uplit stage setting of a recital, accompanied by Marc Mostovoy, founder of The Chamber Orchestra of Philadelphia. Her red dress offered an absorbing challenge, requiring Shanks to include every red oil color available to capture its glow. Even still, it challenges photographers and printers, and demands a visit in person. The painting is now the focal point of the newly re-opened National Portrait Gallery and Smithsonian Museum of American Art in the historic former United States Patent Office building four blocks north of the National Mall in Washington, DC.

"The Recital", (Denyce Graves & Marc Mostovoy)

1999; oil on canvas; 90 1/4 x 54 1/4 inches

National Portrait Gallery, Smithsonian Institution, Washington, DC
Promised gift of Ian and Annette Cumming

In the words of Margaret Thatcher:

"Europe was created by history. America was created by philosophy."

"Success is having a flair for the thing that you are doing; knowing that is not enough, that you have got to have hard work and a sense of purpose."

"Why do you climb philosophical hills? Because they are worth climbing. There are no hills to go down unless you start from the top."

Margaret Thatcher was the longest serving Prime Minister of Great Britain in recent history and was the first woman ever to take the role. Her victory over Edward Heath for leadership of the Conservative Party in 1975 surprised many. In 1979, the Conservative Party won the General Election and Margaret Thatcher succeeded James Callaghan as PM.

She left the House of Commons in 1992, and now sits in the Lords as Baroness Thatcher. Her writings include two volumes of memoirs: The Downing Street Years *and* The Path to Power. *In 1994, she first sat for Nelson Shanks and the two struck up a fast friendship based on mutual respect. "Nelson is a true philosopher," she proclaimed when this portrait, his second of her, was unveiled for the College of William and Mary.*

Portrait of Margaret, The Lady Thatcher

1999; oil on canvas; 40 x 30 inches

Courtesy of the Muscarelle Museum of Art
Collection of The College of William and Mary in Virginia
Gift of J. Bruce Bredin '36, 2000.026

Michael Bloomberg

2002; oil on canvas; 42 x 32 inches

Collection of Johns Hopkins University

William Jefferson Clinton

2005 - 2006; oil on canvas; 90 x 48 inches

National Portrait Gallery, Smithsonian Institution, Washington, DC

"An evangelist for the gospel of the visual arts."

Susan Mansfield, Aberdeen Magazine

Sir Timothy Clifford served as director of the National Galleries of Scotland for 21 years. He extended its collection with large sweeping strokes, acquiring treasures by Botticelli, Raphael, El Greco and Canova for Scotland. He also discovered a Michelangelo drawing worth many millions of dollars in a drawer at the Smithsonian's Cooper-Hewitt, National Design Museum in New York City. Nelson painted him for the National Galleries of Scotland admiring the Botticelli in a book celebrating his choices for acquisition.

Described by Richard Dorment, art critic for The Daily Telegraph, *as "the most naturally gifted museum man of his generation," Sir Timothy is writing a book exploring how the finest metalwork, furniture, and textiles were frequently designed by the great architects, sculptors, and painters, whose contribution has often been overlooked or underestimated. Verrocchio, Uccello, and Botticelli are discussed as forerunners to William Kent, Roubilliac, and Gravelot.*

Sir Timothy Clifford

2006; oil on canvas; 39 x 46 inches

Commissioned by the American Friends of the National Galleries of Scotland for the National Galleries of Scotland

Nelson painted his friend Sir Timothy Clifford for the National Galleries of Scotland admiring the Botticelli that he acquired.

CHARLES EDWARD MORRIS, NINTH EARL SPENCER

(Holding the legible notes for the Westminster Abbey tribute he gave at the service for his sister, Diana, Princess of Wales)

1999; oil on canvas; 64 x 40 inches

Collection of Charles, Ninth Earl Spencer

Althorp, Northamptonshire, England

Part II

Character & Integrity

Character and integrity define both the subjects portrayed and the means of their portrayal. The portraits that Nelson Shanks paints can convey character and integrity because of his capability and insight as an artist. Counter to prevailing trends, he prizes depth of characterization and probing into personality. He relishes the opportunity to study individuals for gesture, indications of attitude, expression, mental state, point of view and sensibility.

In his works, he depicts character through profound application of artistic means—color, line, atmosphere, and shape—achieving an end of unforgettable integrity.

It is Nelson Shanks' firm conviction that whatever can be seen can be conveyed in paint and that whatever can be seen can be felt. With the capability of a master, he challenges the viewer to greater heights of perception. As one critic noted almost a decade ago, "It's good to be reminded how magical painting can be when it's performed by a master magician."

Michael and Arianna Huffington

1996; oil on canvas; 80 x 54 inches

Culver Educational Foundation

Governor John Engler

2005; oil on canvas; 82 x 50 inches

Collection of the State of Michigan

"To be inside the creation of a work of art rather than a passive onlooker is infinitely fascinating...I came away with a new respect for how hard it is, and how some people seem to have a God-given ability to coordinate eye and hand and probe deep beyond the surface."

J. Carter Brown
(on the occasion of sitting for a portrait by Nelson Shanks)

J. Carter Brown

Director emeritus, National Gallery of Art, Washington, DC

1993; oil on canvas; 30 x 40 inches

United States Commission of Fine Arts

LUCIANO PAVAROTTI, (A STUDY)

2004; oil on hardboard; 28 x 20 inches

Collection of the artist

RENÉE FLEMING, (AS RUSALKA BY MOONLIGHT) A STUDY

2006; oil on canvas; 22 x 16 inches

Collection of the artist

Frank Giordano

2006; oil on canvas; 40 x 30 inches

Collection of The Union League of Philadelphia

Beth Dozoretz

2001; oil on canvas; 36 x 48 inches

Collection of Dr. Ronald and Beth Dozoretz

Anne Faulkner Schoemaker

2001; oil on canvas; 44 x 36 inches

Collection of Dr. and Mrs. Hubert J.P. Schoemaker

Dr. Hubert Schoemaker

2003; oil on canvas; 50 x 36 inches

Collection of Dr. and Mrs. Hubert J.P. Schoemaker

Dr. Ralph Snyderman

2004; oil on canvas; 50 x 36 inches

Collection of Duke University Medical Center

Dr. Linton Whitaker

2004; oil on canvas; 50 x 40 inches

Collection of The Children's Hospital of Philadelphia

Jenny Taubman

2001; oil on canvas; 40 x 32 inches

Collection of Ambassador and Mrs. Nicholas Taubman

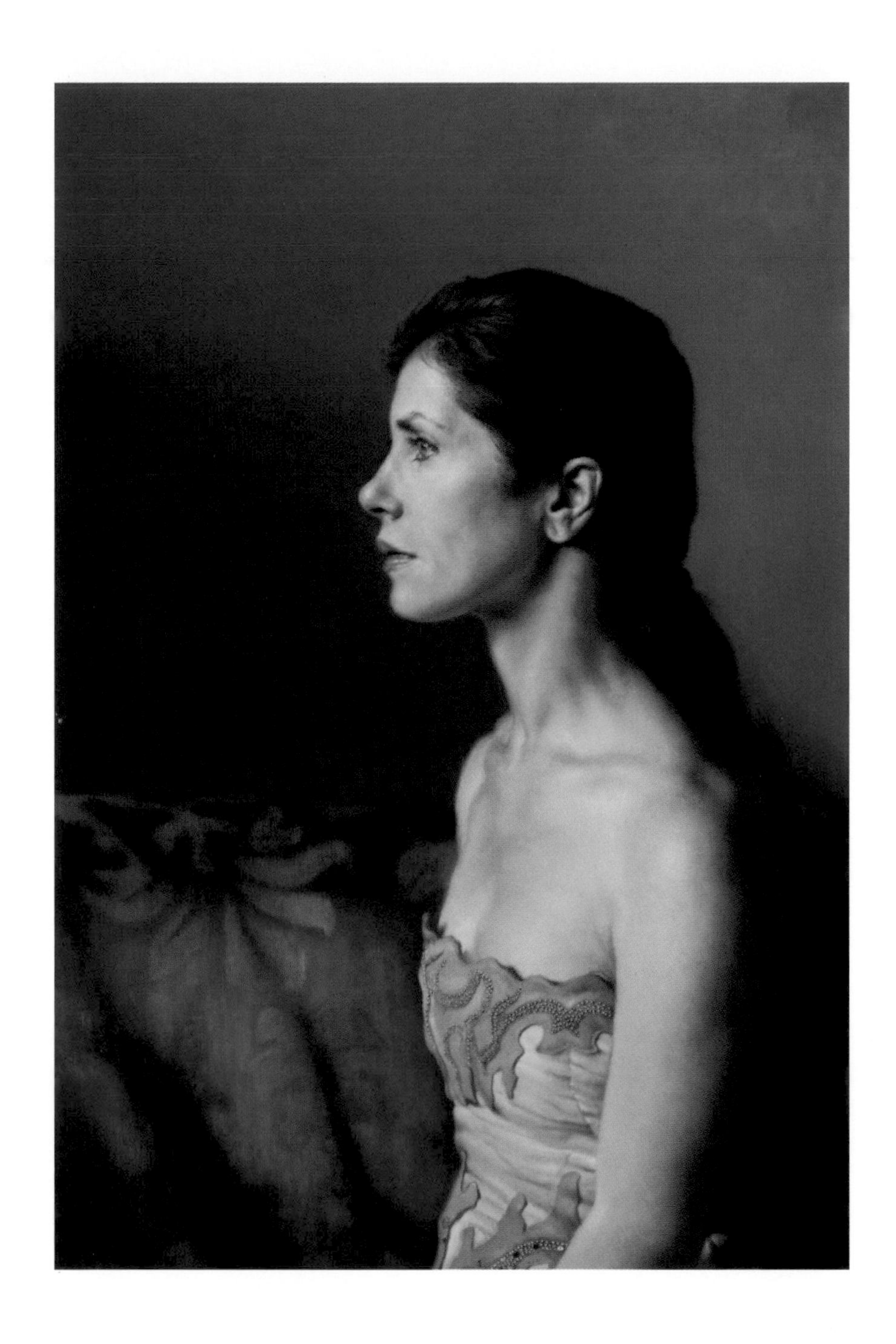

"This painting of Barbara represents my modern day version of the early Renaissance profile portraits, such as those by Polliauolo, Bernardino de Conti, and Ambrogio di Predis."

Nelson Shanks

BARBARA EBERLEIN

2005; oil on canvas; 30 x 20 inches

Collection of the artist

Mrs. Harry Kuch

1992; oil on canvas; 44 x 34 inches

Collection of Arcadia University

Mr. Harry Kuch

1992; oil on canvas; 44 x 34 inches

Collection of Arcadia University

Mary McFadden

1998-2004; oil on canvas; 48 x 36 inches

Larry and Anne Hall Collection

Part III
Metaphor & Meaning

Metaphor and meaning may have even more importance for Nelson Shanks than color, line, shape and atmosphere. He has a way of turning still life into allegorical paintings, which he has defined as groupings of figures or things that evoke a mood or allude to classical or other art, and literature. Even a shadow may assume metaphorical significance. The moods range from solemn to playful.

"The effectiveness of his still lifes, not just as pretty pictures, but as moral allegories, comes from his ability to remove the objects from their traditional context and from our orientation to them. Shanks gives ordinary objects a spiritual or otherworldly import simply by his extraordinary ability to paint and compose…The traditional boundaries of representational painting are often crossed in Shanks' paintings, as it is the artist's goal in all his works to transcend the conventional categories into which we place representational painting. He intends his paintings to function both as definable subjects and as something more elemental," wrote Michael Gitlitz in 1996.

"Your life is only so long. It's important that you use your time to address important issues. You can choose either ignorance about everything beyond your immediate view, or you can try to understand everything about your life, and lives beyond your span. The great artists such as Bach, Beethoven and Shakespeare give us that breadth of vision.

"The painting Hiroshima *represents the victory of the spirit over death, the spirit glimmering as a reflection in the door, and death diminishing as the mandible retreats behind the glass case. There are those who urge me to use my skills to depict the horrors of this world, yet with all due respect, it has been my response to show a shining light rather than bask in the darkness."*

Nelson Shanks

"Hiroshima"

1989; oil on canvas; 28 x 22 inches

The Dayton Art Institute, museum purchase with funds provided by the James F. Dicke Family, 1997.19

"I was compelled to paint realistically, because in so doing I can employ a language we all comprehend, versus gibberish. When you paint realistically and put your own twist on what you see, it opens up a world of powerful metaphorical interpretation.

"In this painting, the angel refers to higher principles, moral and aesthetic, which are under siege. My concern is that we suspend and tether these values for the sake of expediency. What Have We Done to Angels *is, in fact, a crucifixion, the martyr being the angel in a world that has lost its values."*

Nelson Shanks

"What Have We Done to Angels"

1993 – 1996; oil on canvas; 38 x 32 inches

Collection of Jena and Michael King

"Pigtails *with her back to us is facing ahead as we do, increasing our sense of identification in an unexpected way. When the subject faces us, looking in the opposite direction, a direct gaze may be challenging to view. Here we sense that she has paused to listen to us, which creates a feeling of connection. I became absorbed in painting her hair and the subtle shapes that make up her awareness.*

"It's critical that a painter develop the ability to go back and forth, at one level absorbed in the minutiae, but on another level, always stepping back to consider the created whole."

Nelson Shanks

"Pigtails"

2004; oil on canvas; 20 x 28 inches

James A. Michener Art Museum, museum purchase with funds provided by the Janus Society

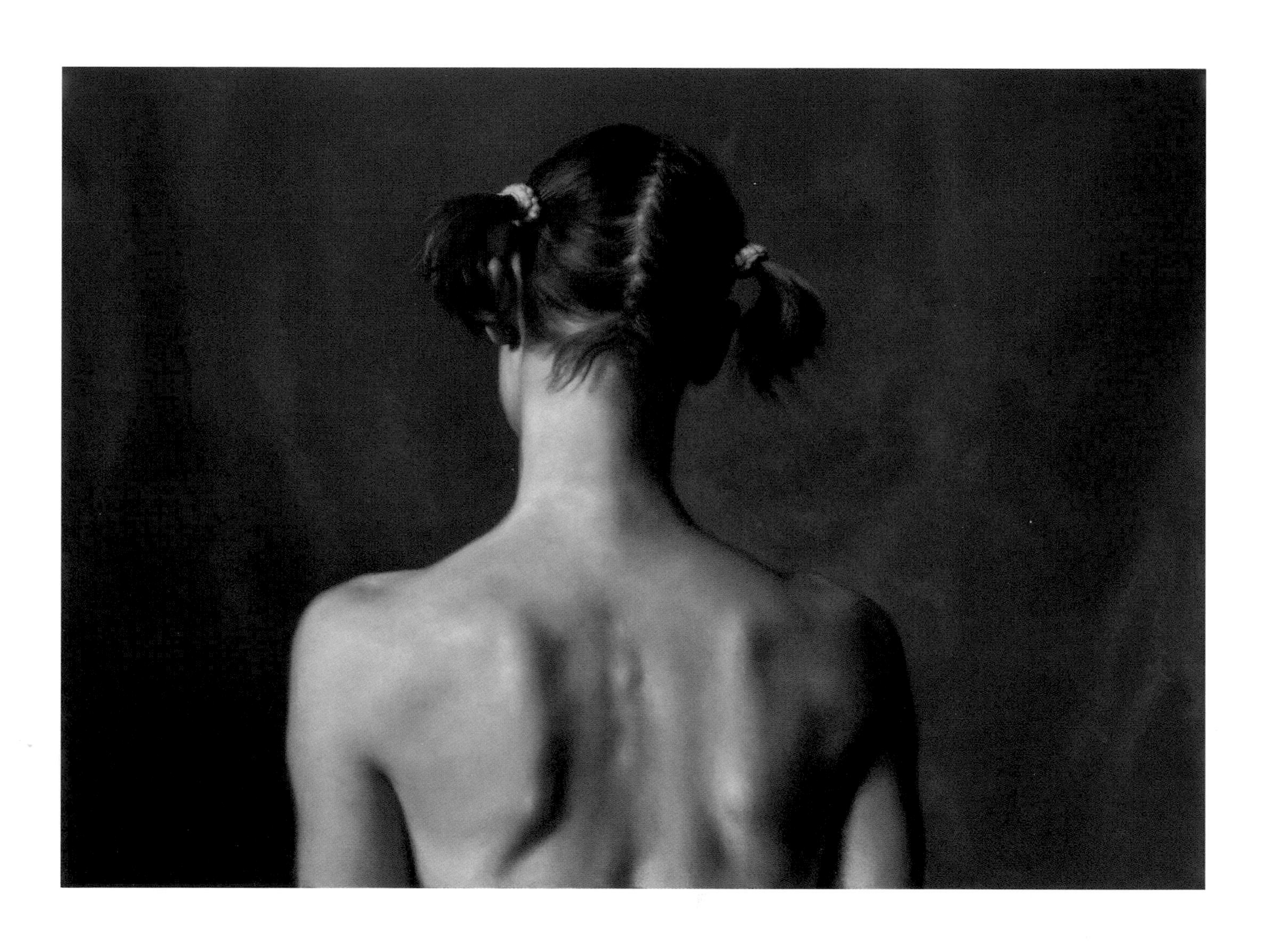

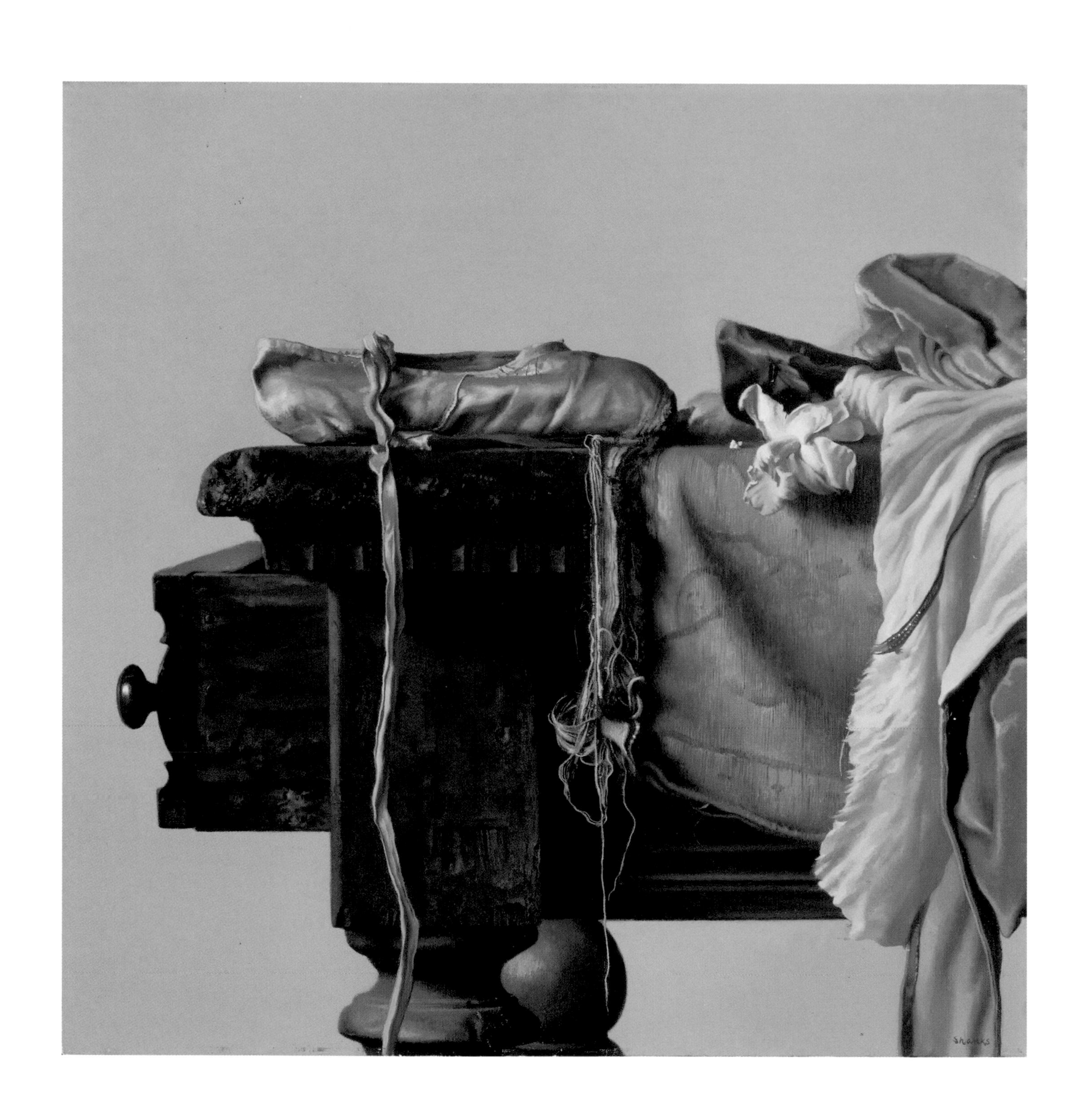

Danilova's Slipper

1977; oil on canvas; 16 x 16 inches

Collection of Dr. Ronald and Beth Dozoretz

"Fox"

2005; oil on canvas; 20 x 24 inches

Collection of the artist

"Woodsprite"

2004; oil on canvas; 29 x 22 inches

Collection of the artist

"I have challenged myself to create artworks with meaning for our times. The dramatic effects of artificial light force careful study of shapes in the abstract. This abstract way of seeing and painting is anything but subjective and accidental, but instead says something about the nature of reality. The headdress comes in and out of focus and the viewer who participates in taking a deeper look is rewarded by the pleasure of recognizing how the appearance of reality is at the same time utterly simple and amazingly complex."

Nelson Shanks

"Psychological effects of dramatic light were explored as early as Caravaggio and his followers in the early 17th century. Other masters of this type of lighting include Bigot, Terbruggen, and Honthorst. The hot artificial lights of our era are even more tantalizing to explore.

"FLORA"

1994; oil on canvas; 34 3/8 x 18 1/4 inches

Collection of Meg Goodman

"THE RECITAL", (DENYCE GRAVES & MARC MOSTOVOY)

1999; oil on canvas; 90 1/4 x 54 1/4 inches

National Portrait Gallery, Smithsonian Institution, Washington, DC

Promised gift of Ian and Annette Cumming

"July Third"

1983 - 1995; oil on canvas; 72 x 30 inches

Collection of the artist

"An aggrandizement of the seemingly mundane, Pumpkin *is a tribute to the majesty of nature.*

"A painting's emotional, intuitive content must be immediate, or it's a flop. I paint to counter the pervasive sense of nothingness to which aspects of today's culture seem to yield, even extol."

Nelson Shanks

"PUMPKIN"

2003; oil on canvas; 20 x 24 inches

Larry and Anne Hall Collection

"Nelson Shanks spent hundreds of hours painting the model Sophia and hundreds more painting the still life that surrounds her. Anthology *is a powerful example in this respect, combining elements of the portrait, nude, and still life. By placing the model, Sophia, in a contraposto stance, Shanks alludes to the classical form, while the objects surrounding her represent to Shanks classical order. As both an artist and an art collector, he is keenly aware of the classical canon both in visual reference and in spirit.*

"If Shanks is to be defined as a classicist at all, it must be a broad definition at whose heart is the focus upon the human form, human ideals, and objects of meaning to our lives."

Michael Gitlitz
Hirschl & Adler Galleries, New York

SOPHIA, (AN ANTHOLOGY)

1993; oil on canvas; 78 x 39 inches

Collection of the artist

SWP

"In contrast to the idealized view of Aristotle Contemplating the Bust of Homer, *I found some gentle humor in the reality of this devoted scholar placing her hand on her canine companion. I did include Homer and a terracotta panel to serve as the window for his contemplation."*

Nelson Shanks

Rembrandt van Rijn
ARISTOTLE CONTEMPLATING THE BUST OF HOMER *(detail)*
Metropolitan Museum of Art, New York

Aggie Underwood

2004; oil on canvas; 44 x 33 inches

Collection of the National Cathedral School

ALEXANDER, (A STUDY)

2004; oil on hardboard; 12 x 10 inches

Collection of the artist

Mr. Fitting

1974; oil on canvas; 16 x 24 inches

Larry and Anne Hall Collection

"Laura's Theme", (A Study in Orange)

2005; oil on canvas; 18 x 24 inches

Larry and Anne Hall Collection

Laura, (A Study)

2004; oil on canvas; 16 x 24 inches

Collection of the artist

"Laura's Theme", (A Study in Blue and White)

2002; oil on canvas; 18 x 34 inches

Private Collection, Boston

"Note the relationship between the color, line and mood in each of these studies. The interpretations may also be to seasons."

Nelson Shanks

"Laura's Theme", (A Study in Red)

2004; oil on canvas; 20 x 20 inches

Collection of the artist

"There is much to be said for humility, trying hard forever. The opinion of the 'art world' is not relevant really, because the greatness of a Vermeer is not related to the transient opinions of 'the experts.'

"Few passages in painting gave me as much pleasure as this knitted hat."

Nelson Shanks

"Mandolin"

2003; oil on canvas; 38 x 34 inches

Private Collection, Connecticut

"BLUEBIRD"

1994; oil on canvas; 20 x 18 inches

Collection of Mr. and Mrs. Randall Presley

MARY

2002; oil on canvas; 22 x 18 inches

Private Collection, Massachusetts

Grace

1996; oil on canvas; 44 x 44 inches

Private Collection, Florida

"From the very real setting of Catalina Island the ghost of horses once raised by its owner emerged. The dreamlike quality of the ghost horse contrasts with its knifelike edges, which are set off in turn by the longer, softer sfumato edges of the far shore.

"Dreams keep me going and I wonder where, today, are the idealists? The Medici shaped society for the better, taking the greatest from former eras and nurturing the artists of their times. Just as the creators of the Renaissance were stimulated by concepts of the classic period, it's our turn to examine the past and bring forward something elucidated for the future."

Nelson Shanks

CATALINA ISLAND

2000; oil on canvas; 34 x 54 inches

Private Collection, California

"Tarot", (Natalie Italiano)
2005; oil on canvas; 28 x 39 inches
Collection of the artist

"In my own education, I had to search out those few painters with something to say about how to see. I absorbed the best of what they had to offer, and developed strong convictions about what works best."
Nelson Shanks

Barbara, (A Demonstration)
2004; oil on canvas; 24 x 20 inches
Collection of the artist

"I am passionate about teaching, about rapidly painted demonstrations of this kind, because I feel a strong personal and social responsibility to draw people to a serious kind of painting that has to do with observation of life."

Nelson Shanks

CONNIE, (A DEMONSTRATION)
2003; oil on canvas; 22 x 18 inches
Collection of the artist

ANNE, (A DEMONSTRATION)
2006; oil on canvas; 20 x 24 inches
Larry and Anne Hall Collection

"I shall even say what it will seem incredible to be told: neither in Italy nor elsewhere was there a real painter to be found...Thus, when the art of painting was dying, more benign stars turned toward Italy, and it pleased God that in the city of Bologna, mistress of science and religion, there arose a most elevated genius, and with him the fallen and nearly extinct art arose again. This genius was Annibale Carracci...."

Giovanni Pietro Bellori, The Lives of the Painters, *1672*

More than four centuries ago the Carracci formed the Accademia degli Incamminati because they judged that the excesses of Mannerism had harmed painting. Scholars judge that their school's revival of study from life altered the history of art, as painters they taught spread knowledge to many cultural centers of Europe throughout the seventeenth century.

In the 21st century, Nelson Shanks believes painting is in need of similar reform. He has painted Incamminati *as a statement of his convictions and as a call to action. In this life-sized work, the friend and model Grace personifies the spirit of painting, striding forward with confidence and purpose toward the future, her fan, a shield and her clutch of brushes, a sword. The anatomical plaster casts in the background allude to painting's foundation in classical tradition, while the manifesto nailed to the wall declares that the time for action is* now.

"We train to become enabled by competence, not restricted by inability."

Nelson Shanks at Studio Incamminati

"INCAMMINATI", (THE PERSONIFICATION OF PAINTING)

2003; oil on canvas; 60 x 40 inches

Collection of the artist

NOW!

INDEX

Part of Nelson's drive to excel as a realist painter was his realization that modern art's claim to show more about reality was "delusional." Nelson painted this "pan" of a still life with objects typical of Cézanne to demonstrate how much was lost, obscured and distorted in Cézanne's attempts to impose a new geometry on observable form. Unlike Cézanne, this painting has, additionally, a subject theme in the selection of objects related to death (the memento mori).

33 Tite Street

1975; oil on canvas; 16 x 12 inches

Collection of Dr. Horace MacVaugh

For more than thirty years, Nelson Shanks has painted meditations on the theme of the victory of the spirit over death, of resurgence, of re-awakening. For today's students of realist painting, the theme of re-awakening has particular resonance, as they seek to learn techniques and knowledge that seemed to be lost and forgotten during the 20th century. Many students see special significance in this small painting titled 33 Tite Street.

On this London street can be found studios for James McNeill Whistler, John Singer Sargent, and Augustus John, among other realist painters. 33 Tite Street was the setting for Nelson Shanks' portraits of Diana, Princess of Wales, and Margaret Thatcher. There Nelson posed a model in the act of awakening. In Center City Philadelphia today, and in cities across the world, Nelson helps open the eyes of students, to be able to see and to convey the meanings that visual reality holds for them.

Bibliography

Bellori, Giovanni Pietro. *The lives of the modern painters, sculptors and architects*. Translated by Alice Sedgwick Wohl; notes by Hellmut Wohl; introduction by Tomaso Montanari. New York: Cambridge University Press, 2005.

Clifford, Sir Timothy. *Choice: Twenty One Years of Collecting for Scotland*. Edinburgh: National Galleries of Art, 2005.

Eichler, Jeremy. "Shostakovich, Profokiev, Britten and Me." *New York Times*. 16 April 2006.

Gitlitz, Michael. "From the Perspective of the Sitter." *Nelson Shanks at the Pennsylvania Academy of the Fine Arts*. Philadelphia: PAFA, 1996.

Hughes, Robert. *The Shock of the New: the Hundred Year History of Modern Art, Its Rise, Its Dazzling Achievement, Its Fall*. New York: Alfred A. Knopf, 1981.

Mansfield, Susan. "The Cultural Evangelist." *Aberdeen Magazine,* 2005. www.aberdeenmagazine.com

Pennypacker, Ramsay. "Portrait of An Artist." *Bucks, The Art, Culture, Lifestyle Magazine*. January/February 2006.

Shanks, Nelson. "A Painter's Progress." *Linea, Journal of the Art Students League of New York*. Summer 2006:10.

Spike, John. "Epilogue." *Nelson Shanks at the Pennsylvania Academy of the Fine Arts*. Philadelphia: PAFA, 1996.

Szozanski, Edward J. "Shanks' Portraits Recall Renaissance Realism." *Philadelphia Inquirer*. 8 November 1996.

Thompson, Dodge. "Portrait of His Holiness Pope John Paul II." *Saint Peter and the Vatican: The Legacy of the Popes*. Alexandria, VA: Art Services International, 2003.

Vengerov, Maxim. "Maestro of the Spirit." *Time Europe*. 11 October 2004. www.time.com.

Carl Weiss designed *Mastery & Meaning*. Body copy has been set in Garamond, a typeface based on the work of 16th century French typographer Claude Garamond. Titles are set in Trajan, a typeface that is based on the lettering displayed on Roman monuments and was created by the designer Carol Twombly for Adobe in 1988. With the exception of *Diana*, which was photographed by Prudence Cummings and *The Earl Spencer*, by Matthew Hollow, paintings have been photographed by Joe Painter and scanned by Boston Photo Imaging. Alcom Printing printed the catalog on 100# Porcelain text and 120# Porcelain cover.